START-UP BASS GUITAR

It's never been easier to start playing bass guitar!

GW00482250

Published by
Hal Leonard

Exclusive Distributors:
Hal Leonard
7777 West Bluemound Road
Milwaukee, WI 53213
Email: info@halleonard.com

Hal Leonard Europe Limited
42 Wigmore Street
Marylebone, London, W1U 2RY
Email: info@halleonardeurope.com

Hal Leonard Australia Pty. Ltd.
4 Lentara Court
Cheltenham, Victoria, 3192 Australia
Email: info@halleonard.com.au

Order No. AM1002914
ISBN: 978-1-84938-982-2
This book © Copyright 2011 Hal Leonard.

Written and produced by David Harrison for shedwork.com
Design by Fresh Lemon.
Photography by Matthew Ward.
Model: Dave Weston.
Edited by Tom Farncombe.
Printed in the EU.

www.halleonard.com

The bass guitar has a lot going for it: it's relatively easy to grasp the basics, it's very versatile, it's straightforward to maintain and crucially bass players are always in demand. Every band needs one, and whether you're into country, pop, rock, jazz, funk or disco, you're bound to find yourself at the heart of a rhythm section before long. This book will guide you through your first steps.

Take the time to make sure you understand the sections on getting started—a little while spent ensuring your posture is up to scratch will prevent you from getting into bad (and painful) habits later on.

If reading music is new to you, be sure to check out the section on reading tablature on page 14—it's not difficult, and will come in very handy. All the exercises in this book are written in conventional notation together with tab, so you can choose to read whichever comes most naturally.

If you don't already own a bass guitar, speak with bass players you know. You'll get a good idea of what to look for and what is likely to be within your price range before you go spending all your hard-earned cash.

You might notice that bass guitars are available with differing numbers of strings—five strings, even six, seven, eight or twelve strings—but all these permutations are extensions of the basic instrument, which has four strings. You should definitely start by buying a four string model, as shown and used in this book.

When it finally comes to buying your instrument, don't go on looks alone: make sure you have someone on hand who can play the bass for you so you can hear how it'll sound played properly. A reputable brand is a good guide but the sound of the bass and its general playability (comfort and ease of use) are the two things to watch out for especially.

And remember—you'll need an amp, too, so leave a chunk of your budget aside for that!

PARTS OF THE BASS GUITAR

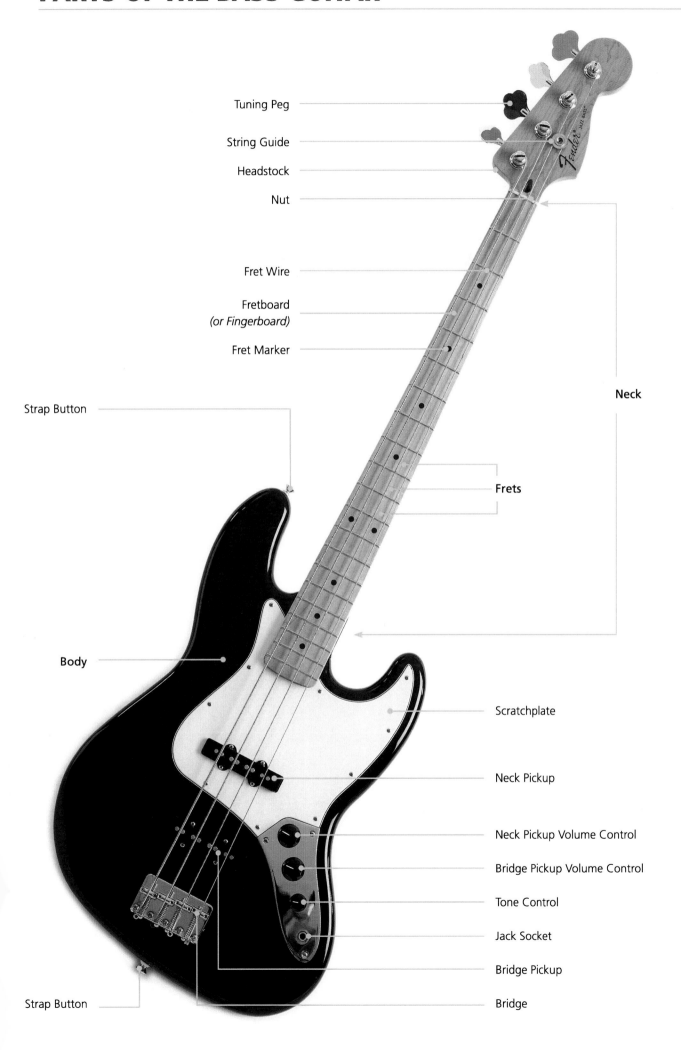

Tuning Peg

String Guide

Headstock

Nut

Fret Wire

Fretboard
(or Fingerboard)

Fret Marker

Strap Button

Neck

Frets

Body

Scratchplate

Neck Pickup

Neck Pickup Volume Control

Bridge Pickup Volume Control

Tone Control

Jack Socket

Bridge Pickup

Strap Button

Bridge

GETTING STARTED

In terms of essential kit, you'll really only need a few things to get up and running with the bass guitar. Apart from the bass and an amp, here are the basic items you should own.

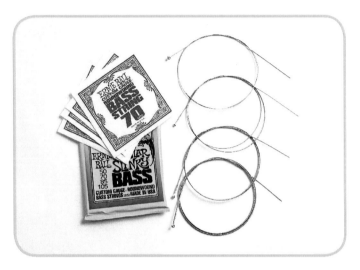

Strings (above): always keep a spare set. You're unlikely to break them, but it's better to be safe than sorry. In any event, when they lose their brightness, it's time to change them.

A cable is a must — and it's worth spending the extra for one that's durable and reliable: you don't want the added hassle of crackles and loose connections.

We'll start by learning how to play with your fingers, but you might like to try using a pick (below) as well. This is explored on page 40.

An electronic tuner is simple to use and very accurate (below).

POSTURE

The bass guitar is a heavy instrument and interaction with it requires some stamina. Good technique begins with good posture, so let's take a look at the options.

If you're standing, be sure to distribute the weight evenly between your feet and adopt a solid stance with your feet wide enough apart to balance easily and spread the load.

You'll need a strap. Although you can buy straps designed for bass guitar, which are wider and sometimes padded to help you handle the weight of the instrument, you'll be fine to start with a regular guitar strap. The strap should be adjusted like so: in a sitting position, attach the strap to the bass and place it over your left shoulder. While holding the bass in your usual (seated) playing position, adjust the strap until it is just taut. Now, when you stand up the strap will hold the bass in the same position relative to your body as it is when you are sitting.

You will probably do most of your practising sitting down. Place the bass on your right thigh. Hold it against your body and let your right forearm rest comfortably on top. Your right elbow should be fairly close to your body.

One thing you'll notice about playing bass in a sitting position is that it is easy to tense up if you are not careful. This can really hurt your playing—if your body is tense, your music will sound tense. Especially while practising, it is important to make a conscious effort to remain relaxed.

HOLDING THE BASS

Once you're sitting (or standing) comfortably, you'll want to make sure you're holding the bass properly: the correct hand positions are the key to comfort and good technique.

RIGHT HAND

Here's a good 'default' position for the right hand: place the tips
of your first two fingers on the bottom (thickest) string, with
the thumb resting lightly on the neck pickup. The thumb, just
touching the bass, will give the hand stability and will serve as a
reliable reference point.

For now, pick the strings firmly up with the tip of the index finger:
experiment with the strength of picking, listening to the difference
in tone (not just volume) that varying amounts of effort and
friction will create. Be sure that the second finger is clear of the
string so the bass can sound clearly.

When playing the other strings, move the fingers across followed
by the thumb. Here (right) the fingers are resting on the third
string and the thumb is now placed on the bottom string. If you
retain this basic position the thumb will stay one string behind the
picking finger.

LEFT HAND

The left hand is placed with the thumb resting behind the neck
on the 'bulge' of the neck profile. The thumb should never be
allowed to drift around towards the upper edge of the neck. With
the thumb in this central position, the fingers are well-supported
and free to find their place on the frets.

Let the fingertips come down onto the strings in a gentle curve,
and without the rest of your fingers making contact with the
strings on the fingerboard or the edge of the neck.

The most important thing to bear in mind here is that the left
hand should at no point be holding the neck in place. All the
support should be provided by the strap, with the left thumb
alone making permanent contact with the neck.

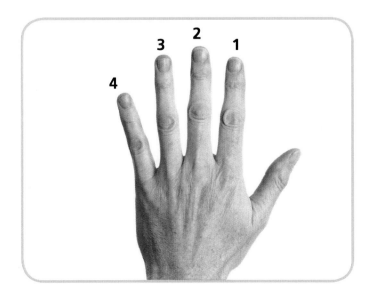

You'll find the left-hand fingers referred
to as 'first', 'second' and so on. They are
numbered as shown, starting with the index
finger (left).

If you're playing left-handed, simply reverse
the instructions in this book that refer to the
right and left hands.

TUNING UP

There are various ways to tune the bass guitar, but they amount to the same thing.

You'll need a reference note or an electronic tuner, and we'll have a look at both methods below.

Just to avoid confusion, it's worth spending a moment on the numbering conventions of the different bass guitar strings. They are arranged in order of pitch (lowest to highest note), with the thickest string also known as the *bottom* string as it has the lowest pitch. The thinnest, with the highest pitch, is also called the *top* string. The strings are also numbered: the top string is the *first* string, down to the bottom, which is the *fourth* string.

TUNING TO THE PIANO

The notes indicated on the piano keyboard below correspond to the four strings of the bass guitar. For reference, the top string tunes to the G an octave and a fourth below middle C.

In fact, music for bass is written *one octave higher* than it sounds to make it easier to read. See the written and actual pitches for the strings at right.

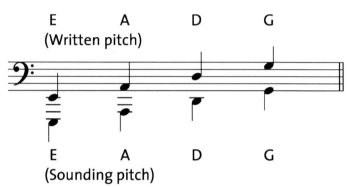

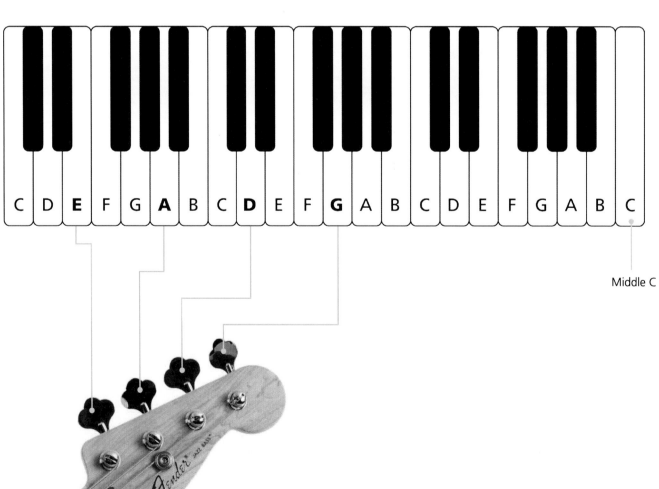

Middle C

Relative Tuning

If you tune the bottom string accurately, you can then use that string to tune the others.

Here's how it works:

- Place a finger on the 5th fret of the bottom (fourth) string—this will give you the note you need (A) to tune the open third string.

- Once that's done, play a note on the 5th fret of the third string. It'll be D, which is the note you need for the open second string.

- And again, play a note on the 5th fret of the second string to give you the note you need (G) for the open first string.

Although it might seem a bit fiddly, this method is great for checking a single string if you're in the middle of playing, and since it relies on your ears it's great training too... check the diagram below for fret positions for each of the reference notes.

Clip-on style tuners are especially convenient (see the section on electronic tuners, below).

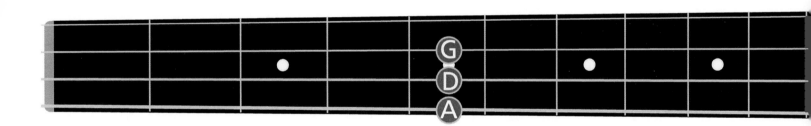

Electronic Tuners

Using an electronic tuner has lots of advantages: they're pretty fool-proof, and very precise.

And, if you're tuning in a noisy situation, plugging a tuner in or attaching it to the bass means you can tune even if you can't hear the bass properly.

Play the bottom string, and the device will show you on its display whether you're low or high.

Tune the string in the right direction and, when it's up to pitch, the display will let you know. Simply move on to the next string and so on, until the instrument is tuned.

YOUR AMP

After your bass guitar, an amplifier will be your biggest purchase—and the combination of amp and guitar will determine the sound you make.

Be sure to shop for an amp with your bass guitar: your sound is a very personal thing and you'll want to hear the two together.

To begin with, you'll need an amp that's powerful enough for band practice and perhaps performing at small venues. The type of amp pictured is ideal for this: it's portable yet sturdy and easily loud enough.

Importantly, it's also specifically built as a *bass* amp. Don't be tempted to use a guitar or keyboard amp as you'll soon damage them. Bass amps are particularly tailored to cope with the low-frequency sounds that your bass creates.

Set the tone on your bass as follows: start by positioning the pickup volume controls to full, with the tone control at halfway.

Then, on the amp, with all the settings at halfway ('twelve o'clock' as pictured below), adjust the master volume control until you're happy with the volume level.

Now use the tone controls on the amp to create the overall sound you're after. It'll take a while to discover what your particular combination of bass and amp can achieve.

PRACTICE

- A little practice every day is much more valuable than a finger-numbing mammoth session once a week.

- Keep a check on your posture and technique, to avoid any niggles creeping into your playing.

- Start slowly and build up: there will be a little wear and tear on your fingers to begin with, and it will take a bit of time to build up the calluses on your fingertips—it's easy to overdo it, especially at the beginning.

- Set a target for each practice session, and make it realistic. Some people keep a practice diary, making a note of things to try in the next session. It's a great way to record your progress.

- Set aside time to play for fun. Keep it separate from your practice time, but make sure you sit and play once in a while for no particular reason: after all, it's why you're learning to play bass!

Practising a little each day is the best way to build up your technique and confidence steadily.

READING MUSIC

Athough you can use standard music notation, many bass guitarists use a customised notation system called tablature, or *tab*.

Tablature is a musical notation system for stringed instruments that shows the performer exactly where to play each note on the fretboard. This notation is either used alongside, or instead, of standard notation, which shows the actual pitches.

If you haven't yet learned to read either system, you should try learning tablature first. It's easier to learn, and it's very common for bass guitar.

The tablature system consists of four horizontal lines, each representing a bass guitar string. The fourth string is the bottom line of the tablature staff, and the first string is the top line.

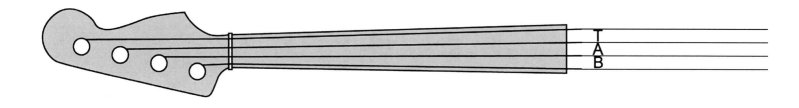

This layout is inverted from the actual string positions on the instrument. Here, the high-pitched notes lie high on the staff and the low-pitched notes lie low on the staff. In this way tablature resembles standard notation.

A number on a line indicates at which fret to depress that string. This example (right) shows a note played on the third string at the 2nd fret. This is followed by a note played on the fourth string at the 3rd fret.

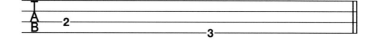

Sometimes, stems and beams above or below the staff denote the rhythm. In this example, the rhythm is a series of eighth notes (see opposite).

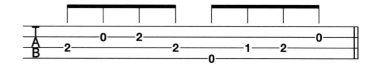

In standard notation, notes are written on a five-line grid called a *staff*.

The *pitch* of the note (how high or low it sounds) determines its position on the staff.

In this book, conventional notation is used alongside tablature, so let's look at the basics now.

We'll pick up more symbols and know-how as we go along, but for now let's look at the way the notes are written on the staff.

Here are the notes, together with their names: the first seven letters of the alphabet (A–G) are used to name the notes.

The curly symbol at the start of the staff is the *bass clef*, showing that the music is pitched for bass instruments.

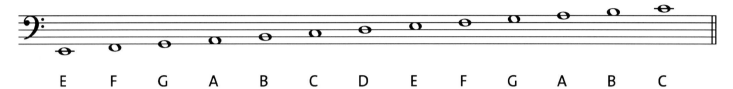

E F G A B C D E F G A B C

The staff is divided into groups of beats called *measures* or *bars* by vertical *barlines*. Reading the rhythm notation is pretty simple. Look at the beginning of a piece of music and you will see the *time signature*.

The number on the top shows the number of beats per measure and the bottom number shows what type of note gets one beat. A 4/4 time signature says that there are four beats per measure and a quarter note gets one beat. This is the most common metre in music.

There are five rhythmic values (kind of notes) that you need to know—whole notes, half notes, quarter notes, eighth notes and sixteenth notes. There are two eighth notes and four sixteenth notes to a quarter note, so in 4/4 an eighth note represents half a beat and a sixteenth note indicates a quarter of a beat.

In the U.K. these rhythmic values are sometimes known by different names, and these are also shown in the diagram below. Notice the *double* barline at the end: these are used to divide sections of music up.

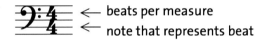

← beats per measure
← note that represents beat

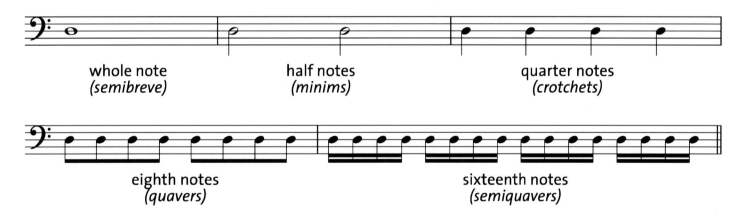

whole note *(semibreve)*   half notes *(minims)*   quarter notes *(crotchets)*

eighth notes *(quavers)*   sixteenth notes *(semiquavers)*

Where no note is played for a specific time value, a *rest* symbol is used. This is how they look:

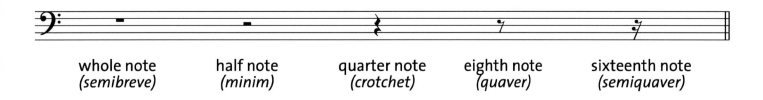

whole note *(semibreve)*   half note *(minim)*   quarter note *(crotchet)*   eighth note *(quaver)*   sixteenth note *(semiquaver)*

THE E STRING

Okay, it's time to get started with the actual business of playing! Let's begin with the bottom string: the E string.

Play the open E string a few times using the right-hand position from page 9.

Play the notes by alternating your 1st and 2nd fingers, trying to make the tone from each even in sound and volume.

By the way, notice the thin-and-thick vertical lines at the end of the exercise. This is a *final* barline, indicating the end of an entire piece.

Count two beats for each note:

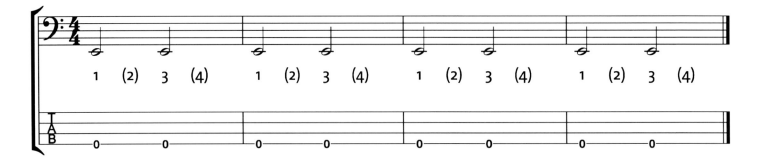

Now place the 1st finger of your left hand on the 3rd fret as shown (right):

This will produce a G, written like so (below):

The next note to try is A, fingered with the 4th finger on the 5th fret of the bottom string (right):

It's written like this (below):

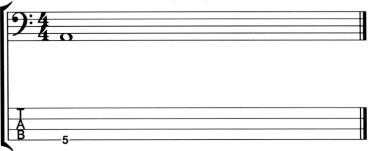

Let's put these three notes together in a simple blues-style bass line. This bass line could be played as a repeated rhythmic phrase, known as a *riff*.

The beat counts are written out below the notes. Try counting the beat out loud to keep a steady flow to the music.

On the opposite page, the rhythm was in half notes. Now we're playing quarter notes. Again, play the notes by alternating between your 1st and 2nd right-hand fingers.

It's also time to introduce fingerings. These are small numbers placed above or below the note head that tell you which finger to use.

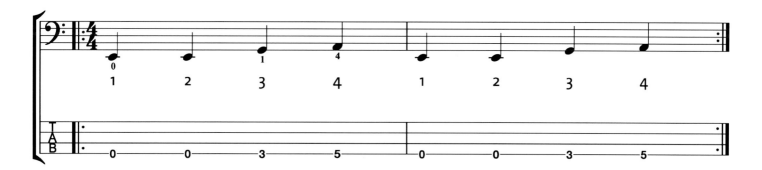

Notice these symbols at either end of the music (right):

These are *repeat barlines*, showing that the music between them should be played twice.

By the way, you might have noticed that the A we're playing is the same note as the open third string. In fact, there's really nothing to stop you playing it that way instead. Which sounds better?

THE A STRING

Let's move on to the A string. We'll
finger the notes the same way, and
learn their names as before.

**This time, play the open third string several times,
ensuring the tone is even and the rhythm is regular.**

Count two beats for each note:

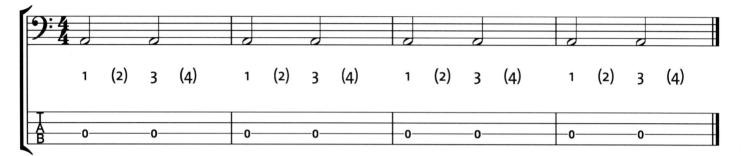

Now place the 1st finger of your left hand on the 3rd fret
of the third string (right):

This creates a C (below):

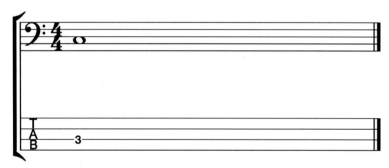

This is D, played on the 5th fret of the third string (right):

Here's how it's written (below):

On page 17 we put the three notes we'd learnt together to make a riff on the E string. Here's the same riff, but this time on the A string:

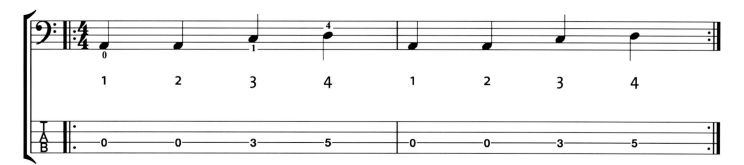

Now it's time to combine the two riffs by moving from the bottom string to the third string and back again. Keep a steady beat throughout, with a consistent tone: the only thing that should change is the pitch.

Don't forget to keep checking that your left-hand thumb is creating the best position for your fingertips when fretting notes by placing it on the back of the neck at the fattest point.

Study the right-hand positions on page 9 again. Start with your right-hand thumb on the neck pickup for the E string riff, played four times.

Then, move your thumb so it rests on the bottom string when you play the riff on the A string; finally, move it back to the pickup when you return to the E string riff for the last two bars.

Keep alternating your 1st and 2nd fingers to play the notes. Changing cleanly from one string to the next will take practice, so start slowly and get it sounding good before trying to speed up.

Try to play this exercise from memory instead of reading—you'll have much more energy to listen to the sound you're making. And after all, that's the most important thing!

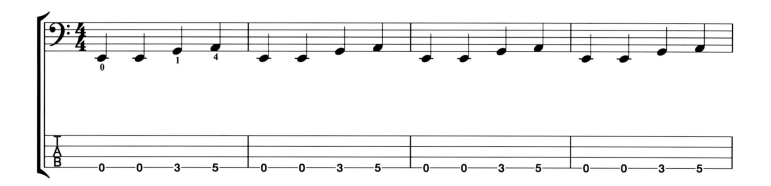

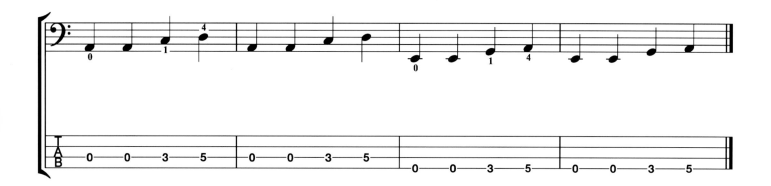

MOVING THE RIFF

We've already seen how, by moving to another string, we can change the pitch of a musical phrase. Now we'll expand this idea by playing elsewhere on the neck.

First of all, take a look at this phrase. It's the same riff as before, but this time all the notes are fretted, starting on B:

The notes are B, D and E. They are the same distance relative to each other as in the previous two versions of the riff, so the melody sounds the same, but it starts two frets higher than the riff on A. So let's see what happens if we just play everything two frets higher on the same string.

Let's check the fingering for each note. The B is played with the 1st finger on the 2nd fret of the third string (right). The D is up on the 5th fret, so move the 1st finger up (below left); this leaves the 4th finger free to play the E on the 7th fret (below right).

This isn't a very efficient or comfortable way of playing the riff, so let's look at the alternatives.

In fact, we can play the whole riff on the first couple of frets. Play B as before, using the open second string to play D, and finger the second string at the 2nd fret to play E (right). Use your 1st finger on the left hand to play each fretted note.

Here's how the tab looks now:

Now here's another option. Start with B played with the 3rd finger of the left hand on the 7th fret of the bottom string (below left):

Move to D and E on the third string as in the first example on the opposite page (below right). The 1st finger is on the 5th fret.

This way, all the notes are in easy reach, and the same pattern can be played elsewhere on the neck, too.

Placing the first finger at the 5th fret puts that hand in 'fifth position'.

PUTTING IT TOGETHER

Now that we've learnt to play the riff in various different places, let's play it in a sequence of twelve bars, known as a 12-bar blues.

Most blues songs use this format, and once you learn a blues bass line it's often just a case of tweaking it a little to fit different blues songs.

We'll also look at *first* and *second time* bars.

Remember how the repeat signs tell you to play a section twice? Well, this time there's a different ending for each time through. On the first play-through, play the bars

within the horizontal bracket numbered '1': that's the *first time* bar. On the repeat, play the *second time* bar, numbered '2'.

Notice how the riffs starting on A and B are played in more than one position, as discussed on pages 20–21. At the beginning of the first time bar, where the two riffs are played next to each other, it makes most sense to play the B riff in a position that allows a simple two-fret move down to the A riff.

Elsewhere, however, it's just as easy to play the riffs using open strings. You'll start to get a feel for it with practice.

You will often find that there's more than one logical place to play a series of notes and generally you'll be guided by what you're playing either side of a particular phrase.

Now let's think about some simple variations that can be made to the bass line, taking the E riff as an example. First of all, try playing the quarter notes as pairs of eighths. To help keep a steady beat, count "one and two and" etc. out loud as shown:

Remember to keep alternating your right-hand fingers!

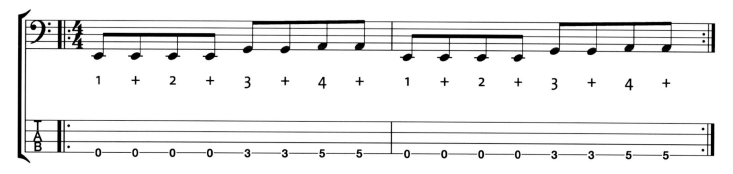

Next, we'll stay on the first note for a beat-and-a-half. The quarter note has a dot added, which extends its value by half (right).

Dots can be used on any simple note value to increase the duration in this way. A half note, for example, that would normally be worth two beats, is worth three beats as a dotted half note (right).

Count as shown, with the "and two" under your breath:

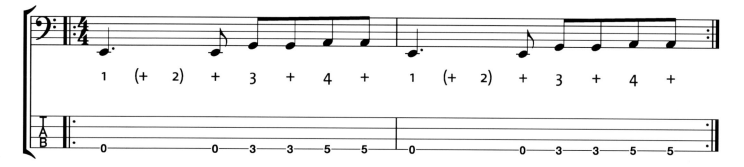

PLAYING WITH THE DRUMMER

It's worth mentioning at this point that everything you do as a bass player in a band is going to be very closely linked to the other musicians that you're playing with, and in particular the drummer.

The bass player provides a link between the harmony of chordal instruments (such as keyboards and guitars) and the rhythms of the drums, so the bassist occupies a pivotal point in any band.

The rhythmic patterns you play should often lock into the drummer's kick drum pattern, either playing an identical rhythm or a complementary one. You need to be keenly aware of what is going on around you!

Listen to your favourite records and listen carefully to what the bass line of the song is, and how that fits with the drum part. Usually you'll hear how they have a very close relationship.

THE MAJOR SCALE

Lots of music uses notes from a *scale*—a sequence arranged in order of pitch. On the bass, learning scales is easy and very useful.

Music that uses notes from a scale is said to be in the *key* of that scale.

One common scale is C major, so-called because it begins on C and contains a squence of notes arranged a particular distance apart (see below).

Take a look at the example below and notice how some of the notes are a *tone* (two frets) from their neighbouring notes, whilst others are just a *semitone* (one fret) apart. The interval spanning C to the next C, by the way, is an *octave*.

C MAJOR SCALE

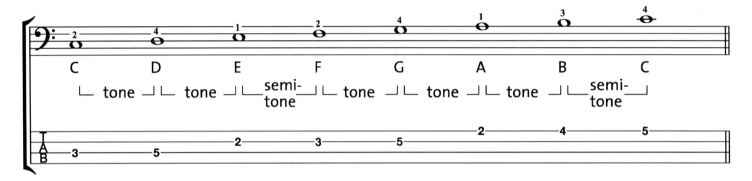

In a major scale, the sequence of intervals (gaps) is always *tone, tone, semitone, tone, tone, tone, semitone*. Learn this sequence, as it will come in handy.

Notice that the interval between E and F, and between B and C, is only half that of the interval between other neighbouring notes. In the musical system, E to F and B to C are just a semitone.

Beginning on C and playing alphabetically through the notes naturally creates the correct sequence of intervals for a major scale.

Note the left-hand fingering, showing that you'll use all four fingers to fret this correctly. All of the notes of the scale fall into a single hand position. A series of fret positions for a scale is called a *scale pattern*.

C MAJOR ARPEGGIO

The different notes of a scale are referred to by their position. In the C scale above, E is the third note. We'd refer to E as the *third* of C, or A as the *sixth*, and so on. Play these notes (below). They're the *root* (first note), third and fifth of C major, up to the next C and back down.

Together they make up the chord of C major, and when they're played one after another like this, it's known as an *arpeggio*. Arpeggios are useful to learn, since bass players often play notes of chords to fit in with the music. We'll talk more about chords in a little while.

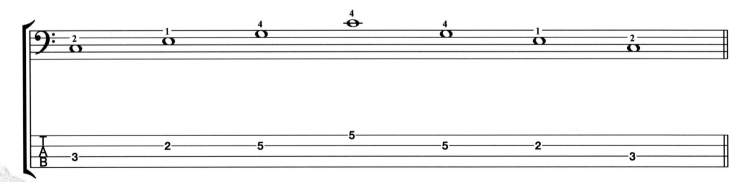

Playing the notes alphabetically starting on a different note than C won't create the *tone, tone, semitone, tone, tone, tone, semitone* sequence of a major scale, so some adjustment is necessary.

Let's take a look at G major, for example (below).

Remember that the interval between E and F is a semitone? At this point, between the sixth and seventh notes, the scale requires a tone. To achieve this, the F is raised by a half step. F is played a fret higher—this is known as *sharpening* the note, shown by the # (sharp) symbol before the note. It's an F#.

G MAJOR SCALE

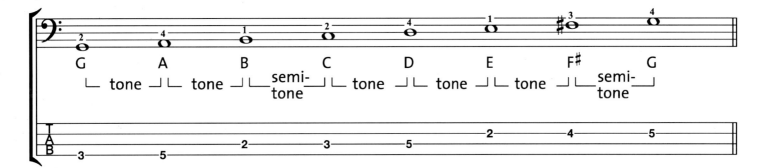

Music in the key of G, therefore, will contain F#. Some keys require certain notes to be lowered (flattened) by a half step, using the ♭ (flat) symbol. Take a look at the next scale. It uses the same scale pattern as G major, but starts on the note one fret below B—B♭. The B♭ major scale uses two flats, B♭ and E♭.

Notice how the finger pattern for the G major scale is the same as C major—it's simply been moved down a string.

B♭ MAJOR SCALE

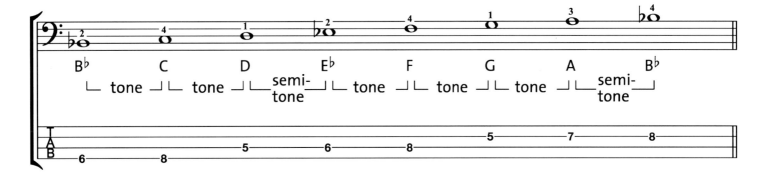

By placing this scale pattern in different positions up and down the neck, and on different strings, we can play any major scale we like.

Remember: alternate your right-hand fingers for these scales, and move your thumb position as you change strings.

KEY SIGNATURES

Every key uses a different number of either sharps or flats. It's common to write the sharps or flats in a key at the start of a piece of music, right after the clef. This is known as the *key signature*, and is a good way to find out the key of a piece.

Music in G major, for instance, will have a # sign on the F line, while a piece in B♭ will have ♭ symbols on the B line and the E space (right).

G major   B♭ major

UNDERSTANDING CHORDS

If you've seen a guitarist strumming several strings at once, he'll have been playing *chords*. Bass players don't play chords, but they need to understand what goes into them.

Bass players are often left to rely on nothing more than *chord symbols* to work out the best note to play at any particular point.

Successfully negotiating chord symbols requires a little theory, some practice and some quick thinking!

In the previous section we had a glimpse of an arpeggio— the basic chord notes played in sequence. Playing arpeggios is a good way to practise playing chord notes.

Let's look at a few more. These are arpeggios of major chords. Some have sharps (♯) or flats (♭) added to create the correct intervals.

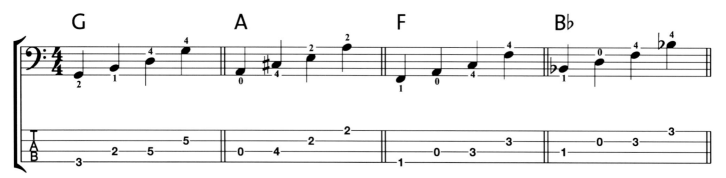

Notice that all these arpeggios use the same pattern, played in different places—and on different strings. Each one has the root, third, fifth and octave. The chord indicated by the chord symbol in each case will contain the root, third and fifth of the scale: this is what guitarists and keyboard players play in various combinations.

Now let's look at another type of chord: the *minor* chord.

Compare the notes in the following arpeggios, and you'll notice that in the minor version (indicated with 'm' in the chord symbol) the third is a half step lower than in the major version. In fact, that's the only difference between major and minor chords.

On the bass, it makes sense to alter the pattern to play the minor arpeggio in the most efficient way.

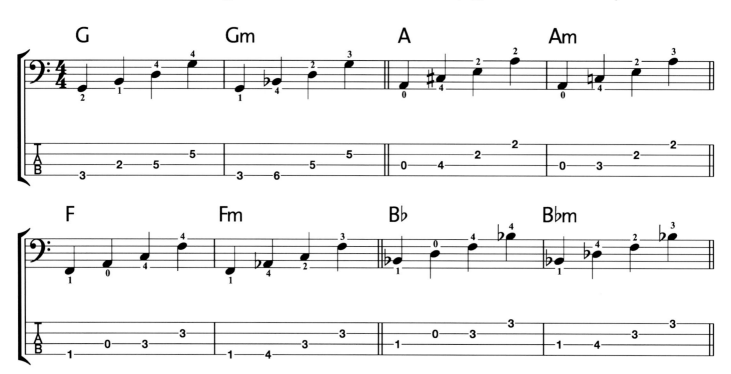

By the way, the *natural* sign (♮) in the Am bar neutralises the previous ♯.

Now that we've got basic major and minor chords sorted, let's take a look at some variations that use *sevenths*. These are other notes added to the chord that change its 'colour'. Sevenths come in two types. They're worth getting to know since they appear in all types of music.

The major seventh is simply the seventh note of the major scale, and in a chord symbol it's written maj⁷ (jazz musicians sometimes use △). Lowering this major seventh a half step gives what's known as a flattened seventh—more usually simply called 'seventh'. It's written as ⁷.

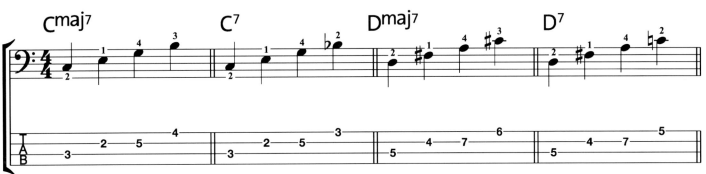

Minor chords, too, can have a ⁷, and (rarely) a maj⁷. Sixths are also commonly included in both major and minor chords.

The job of the bassist is most often to provide a solid rhythmic foundation using notes that underline the chord sequence.

This generally means playing the root of the chord and—as we're about to see—the fifth. The third of the chord distinguishes it as either major or minor, so it's also commonly included in bass lines.

Between them, the root, third and fifth will occupy you 95% of the time, so be sure to get these simple major and minor chord patterns under your fingers!

ALTERNATING BASS

One of the most important techniques for all bass players is *alternating* bass.

It's perfect for country, folk and simple rock styles, but it will come in handy in pretty much every genre.

As the name suggests, alternating bass is all about switching from one bass note to another and back again. This provides interest in simple rhythms.

Let's have a glimpse at the theory behind it and then we'll get on and play through some real-world examples.

As mentioned in the previous section it's common for the bassist to play the root note of the chord.

For variation, the bassist might alternate from the root to the fifth. It creates interest, helps drive the rhythm along and underlines the chord. Take a look at these examples below:

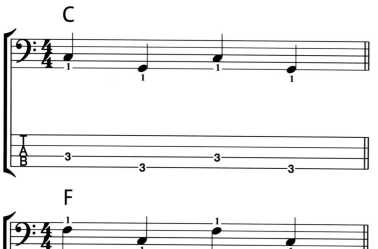

With a chord of C, the root note is C and the fifth is G. Here, the bass line alternates between a note on the third string and a note on the *string below on the same fret*. This is a good general rule for alternating bass.

In this example, on a chord of F, the bass line alternates between the root (F) and the fifth (C). Notice that the pattern is the same: alternating between the root note and a note on the next string down, on the same fret.

When the root note is played on the lowest string, it's impossible to alternate to the next string down, since there isn't one.

In this case, the pattern is as follows: the fifth is located one string higher—and two frets higher—than the root.

In this next example, the root (G) is played in two places, an octave apart—either side of the fifth (D).

In fact, the higher G could be played on the open top string and the D could be played on the open second string. But they're both fingered here in the appropriate place to preserve the patterns we've already looked at.

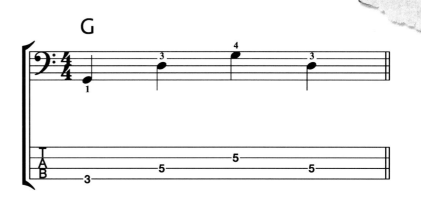

To recap—go from the root to the fifth on alternating beats. Locate the fifth using one of the following methods:

- move one string down, on the same fret as the root, or

- move one string up, and two frets higher than the root.

In the next example, over three different chords, the two methods are combined. In bar 3 both approaches are used, with the root played in different octaves.

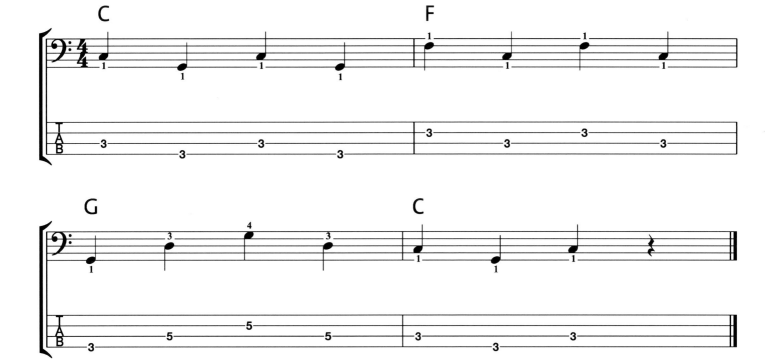

When you play two notes at the same fret on two strings, make sure you finger each note separately with your left hand. use the same finger for both notes but don't try to 'bar' across the two notes at once.

PASSING NOTES

Finding ways of joining root notes from different chords is all part of the fine art of bass playing. One common technique is to use *passing* bass notes.

Passing notes are used momentarily on the way from one note to another.

They're very useful and—as we'll see—not at all difficult to learn.

For a bit of variety, let's look at an example in 3/4. Passing bass notes can be used in 4/4 too, of course, but it's nice to have a change! Imagine a fairly up-beat tempo with a strong first beat of the bar, and count '**one**-two-three **one**-two-three...'.

You should have a rhythm reminiscent of a waltz. In this example, we have four chords in the key of C that you might often see together, one bar for each. For now, just play the root of each chord, counting the beats steadily out loud as you go:

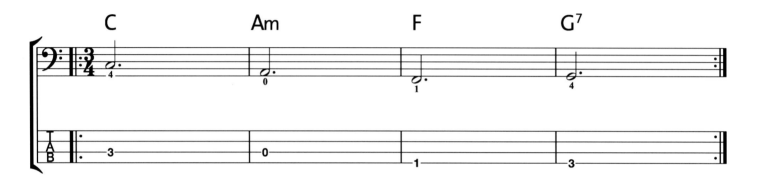

Notice how far apart the first and second chords are. The root notes are next-but-one to each other in the scale of C. They're said to be a *third* apart. Likewise, the distance from A to F is a *third*.

When roots are a third apart, it's simple to join them together by using the 'missing' note of the scale. C and A are joined by B, and A and F are joined by G. Let's play these *passing* notes on the third beat of the bar:

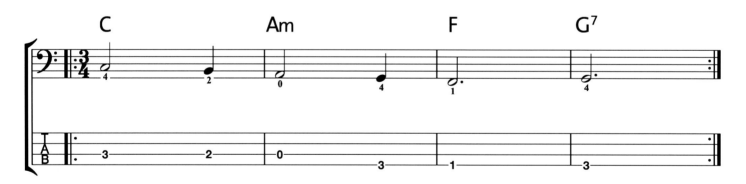

The passing bass notes provide a bit of rhythmic interest, too, but they also highlight a typical bassist's dilemma: the first two bars flow nicely in step, because the roots are a third apart, but then there's no such convenient opportunity for a passing note between bar 3 and bar 4. The rhythmic pattern is abruptly altered.

It would be better to find a note to add at the end of bar 3, just so we continue with the same rhythm. Let's consider some choices.

For a start, you could join them by moving in half steps. This is known as *chromatic* movement (right).

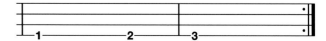

Alternatively, here's an option that's actually not a passing note at all, since it's not between the F and the G: this one follows the 'note above' rule: approach a root by playing the scale note above (right).

It's part of the scale (it's even part of the chord of F) and the effect is similar to that of the first and second bars, where the passing notes descend to the next root note.

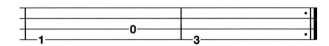

Or, casting your mind back to the *alternating bass* technique, you could use the alternating note for G (that's D), as we know it fits well with G (right):

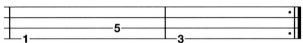

Since this exercise has repeat marks, we'll be returning to C. So how to move to it from G? Well, again there are plenty of options. The simplest solution is to play B (right).

It's in the chord of G and it leads nicely back to C as it's only a half step away. Listen to the way it steps smoothly back up to C.

In fact, it's an example of the 'note below' rule, approaching a root by the note below it in the scale.

NUMBERING CHORDS

By the way, the chords used in these exercises might remind you of a song you've heard. This sequence is one of the most common chord progressions in all popular music.

Because sequences reappear in different guises in lots of songs, musicians have a shorthand way of referring to them. Using the positions of the root notes within the scale of C, we might call this sequence a 'one-six-four-five'. That would be enough information for a whole rhythm section (piano, guitar and bass) to play these four chords.

Traditionally, numbered chords are always written using Roman numerals. The correct way to write this sequence, therefore, would be I-VI-IV-V. You're bound to come across it again sooner or later.

WALKING UP AND WALKING DOWN

In alternating bass style, it's often useful to extend the passing bass note technique to include scale fragments. They join the notes up and provide a bit of interest in the bass line.

We'll use the scale pattern we already know for these exercises. So take another look at pages 24–25 to familiarise yourself with the patterns before we get started.

Now try the G major scale played in eighth notes—two notes per beat. Count "one and two and" etc.

These scale fragments are known as walk-ups and walk-downs, depending on the direction taken to move from one root to the next.

Let's take a look at some typical examples that will give your bass lines that authentic touch.

Notice also the *key signature* at the start of the music, with one sharp, which shows that we're in the key of G.

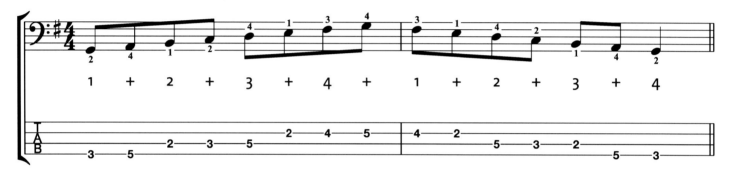

It's often more comfortable to play notes a fifth apart with your 1st and 4th fingers rather than the 2nd and 4th.

Here's a typical I-IV-V-I alternating bass sequence in the key of G. It uses quarter notes: one note per beat.

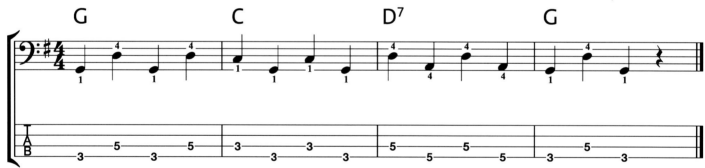

Now, let's walk up in eighth notes from beat 3 of the first bar to the start of the 2nd bar. G to C, going up, is an interval of a *fourth*.

We're using eighth notes so that we have time to walk from G to C. Quarter notes would take longer than we have available and we wouldn't get to C on time. Eighth notes also create a feeling of moving forward.

However, this walk-up only needs two intermediate notes, A and B. So we must be sure not to start walking up too soon, otherwise we'll get to C to early. For this reason, the walk-up has been delayed by playing G twice.

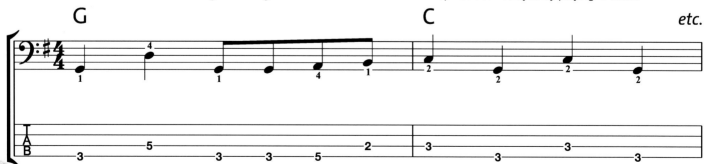

Now let's look at the move from bar 3 to bar 4. We need to walk from D to G, and this time we're walking down.

This time, since we're moving across the interval of a *fifth*, the walk begins right on the third beat and arrives safely on G at the start of the next bar:

Okay, we're going to need something to get us from C to D to keep the rhythm pattern consistent. Strictly speaking, the interval doesn't need a walk-up or -down, but we'll construct something that gives us the feel of the other

transitions. Here's a suggestion that creates the right rhythm and lands on D at the right time. It goes down, and then chromatically up. It looks a bit convoluted, but it's a solution you'll hear commonly played in country music.

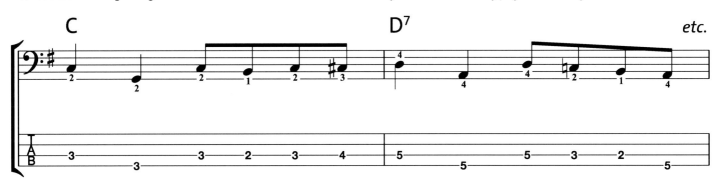

So here's how the whole thing might look now:

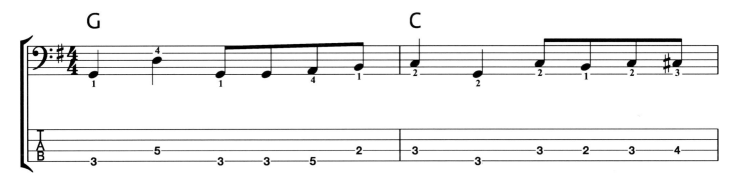

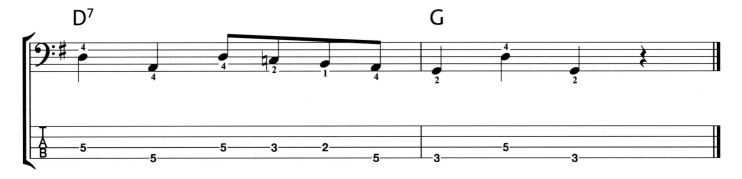

UP OR DOWN?

We walked up a fourth, and down a fifth. You could go in either direction, actually, but bear in mind that while going *up* from G to C, for instance, is a fourth, when you go *down* from G to C you'll be going down a fifth.

You'll need to adjust your timings accordingly. C to A, which is a third descending, becomes a sixth if you go up instead. You'll soon develop a sense of how long you need to walk in either direction for different intervals.

WALKING BASS

Developed from walking up and down, *walking bass* is a technique widely used in swing and jazz styles. The key features here are (i) one note per beat and (ii) a constantly moving bass line.

We'll combine most of what we've already studied thus far to create some authentic walking bass lines that will open up all sorts of opportunities.

Let's start with a typical jazz sequence: I-VI-II-V. And just for a change, let's play in the key of F.

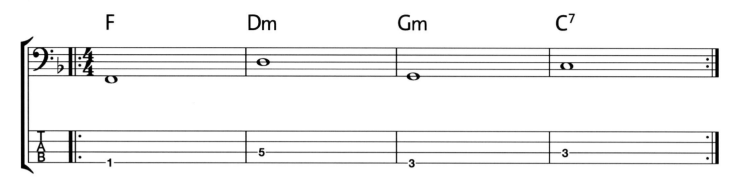

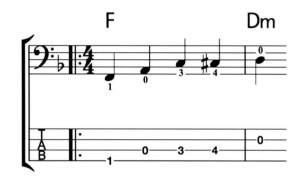

To begin with, play through these suggestions for the first bar moving into bar 2.

The first example uses an arpeggio of F for the first three notes, then a chromatic move up on the 4th beat, to arrive at D at the start of the following bar.

Alternatively, here's an octave jump that leads chromatically down.

There are plenty more options, which you'll no doubt begin to find for yourself as you start to mess about with this sequence. The two shown here, however, are among the most popular ways to move up a sixth in this style.

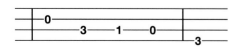

The simplest way to move down a fifth is to walk straight down the scale (left).

Again, you might discover another option that you prefer. You could try playing an arpeggio down (for Dm that's D, A and F) with a chromatic move up to F♯ on the 4th beat; or perhaps an arpeggio up (D, F, A) with a chromatic note down (A♭) on beat 4.

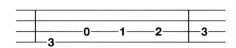

For bar 3, here's perhaps the most obvious solution to move up a fourth. Walking stepwise up the scale would get us to the root of C a beat early, so we need to put in a chromatic note that delays our arrival by a beat.

Remember: walking up or down a *fifth* requires no adjustment. There are three linking steps and they fit naturally in the three beats available. Walking up or down a *fourth*, on the other hand, requires a delay of one beat.

Here's the whole thing:

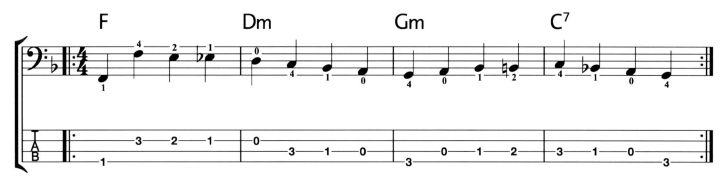

In jazz music, the chords often change every two beats. At that speed, our sequence wouldn't give us time to walk as such, but we can easily resurrect the 'note above' and 'note below' rules we first saw on page 31.

A single note preceding a new root is called an *approach note*. Try this exercise. It changes chord every two beats and uses chromatic approach notes for an authentic jazz feel. Some are from above, others from below.

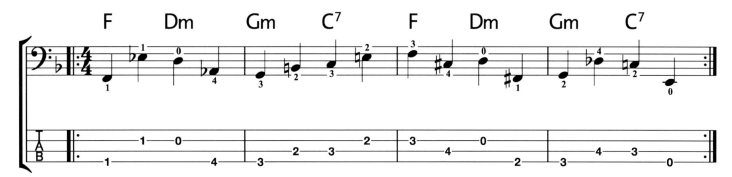

As you can hear, the chromatic approach notes create a radically different sound. You might prefer to temper the style slightly by using notes of the scale (so called *diatonic* notes) to approach the roots rather than going all-out with chromatic movement.

Try to find different places on the fretboard to play this bass line, and experiment with combinations of approach notes. The I-VI-II-V sequence is very common in jazz—you'll soon come across them if you start playing jazz standard tunes.

Get used to finding I-VI-II-V sequences in different keys, too. You should eventually be able to pick them out in any key and provide a solid accompanying bass line at a moment's notice.

BASS STYLES

It's time now for a brief exploration of various popular music styles. As a bass player, you're likely to be called upon to sit in with a band at any time—and you should be prepared!

We first talked about the 12-bar blues on page 22, and how to number chords on page 31. The 12-bar blues is useful sequence to learn, so let's start by outlining the chords for a typical progression.

We'll begin by looking at the blues. It's a huge topic on its own and we'll just scratch the surface.

But the examples on the following pages will stand you in good stead as you take your first steps to becoming a versatile and reliable bassist.

$$\|: \quad I \quad | \quad I \quad | \quad I \quad | \quad I \quad | \quad IV \quad | \quad IV \quad | \quad I \quad | \quad I \quad | \quad V \quad | \quad IV \quad | \quad I \quad | \quad V \quad :\|$$

And here's how it might be in the key of G. This exercise uses a straightforward rock 'n' roll riff over two bars, moved to a new position for each change of chord. Notice, by the way, how the

riff is modified in bar 4 with the addition of a flattened seventh (F♮)—the resulting chord, G⁷, helps 'pull' the music towards the new chord of C.

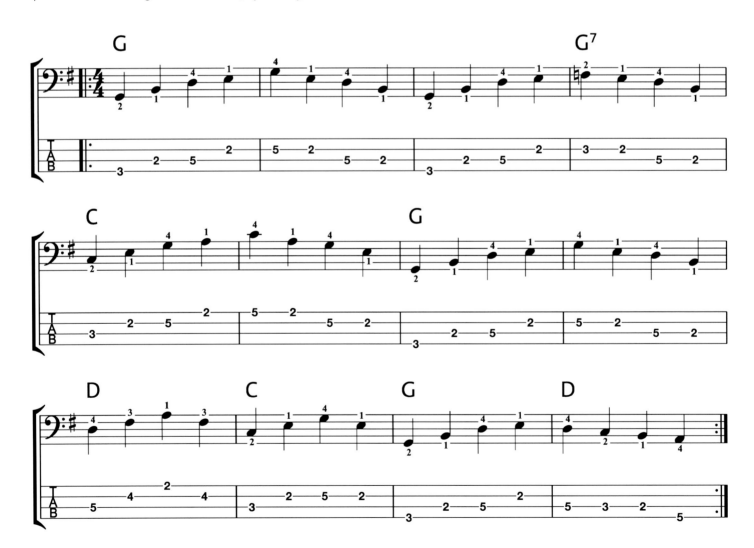

You'll encounter endless variations on this sequence—and not just limited to the blues. The 12-bar form appears in pop, rock, jazz, funk... so it's worth memorising.

Back on page 22 we played through a minor blues. It fits the format we've just examined, but the chords in it are minor since the key of that piece is E minor. Let's look at another minor blues riff:

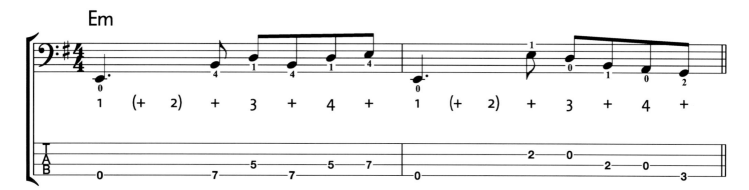

You can easily move this riff about to fit the 12-bar chord sequence, and shorten or modifiy it as you like for bars 9 and 10.

By the way, this riff has the same rhythm as the one at the bottom of page 23. But let's look a bit more closely at eighth notes: how they can be played to create *swing*.

SWING EIGHTH NOTES

Standard eighth notes divide the beat into two equal parts giving an even, solid rock feel (right). We count "1 and 2 and" etc.

However, sometimes the beat is split into three. Eighth notes are bracketed in groups of three called triplets (right). Traditionally they are counted "1 and a 2 and a" etc.

In fact, triplets are often used as the basis of *swing*. Swing is a rhythmic feel in which two standard eighths are used to split the beat unevenly. The first eighth takes on the first two parts of the triplet, and the second eighth is worth just the last part of the tri plet. You could write it like this (right):

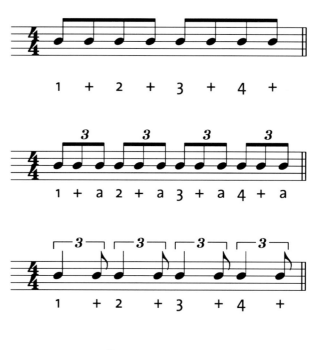

But it's more commonly written with 'straight' eighths with a *metronome marking* above the music to let you know that the eighths are *swung* (right). Although they appear even, these eighths should be played by lengthening the first eighth and shortening the second eighth in each pair.

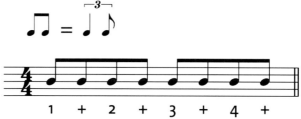

The actual amount of swing you apply is up to you—it'll depend partly on the tempo (speed). And when you're working with a drummer, you'll soon develop an understanding together.

Now go back over some of the eighth note exercises so far (on pages 23, 32–33 and at the top of this page), playing them with swung eighths. Tweak the degree of swing by adjusting the length of the first eighth in each beat.

TURNAROUNDS

One aspect of the 12-bar progression worth special consideration is the end section, where the music 'turns around' to prepare for the next verse. In fact it's known as the *turnaround*. Bass players generally have a repertoire of phrases to play in the last two bars of a blues sequence. Let's play through a couple:

This first one is simply a variation on the ending for the blues on page 36. The final bar begins with a pair of eighth notes. In practice, you might play these as swung quavers or you might play them precisely as written depending on the feel you're after:

For the same blues, you could just put in a walking bass-style I-VI-II-V. It'll give your blues a jazz flavour which might be just what you're after.

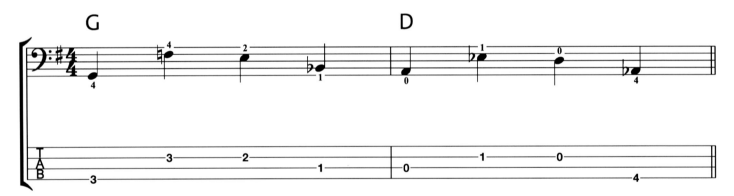

For the final verse you'll probably end on I which in this key is G. It's time to play through one of the all-time classic blues endings.

The > symbol is an accent. Play these notes with more emphasis than normal.

THE BLUES SCALE

When playing a minor blues, soloists often improvise using notes from the so-called blues scale. Bass players can use this scale too, to construct great-sounding bass lines in minor keys.

Since so much popular music stems from the blues, it's a scale that's relevant over a wide variety of genres. Here's the scale in the key of E minor. It's very easy to play on the bass, making use of the open strings:

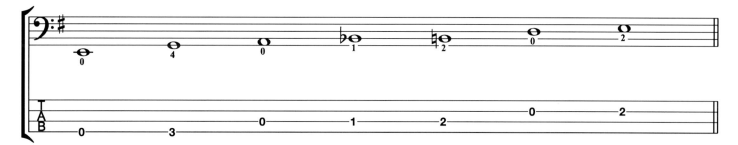

And here it is in action, in a slow blues-rock type riff. You can hear how the B♭—the *flattened fifth*—helps to create a tense, dark atmosphere:

Use the fingering above to play this riff. check back to the guide on page 15 if you're unsure how to count the sixteenth notes here.

By the way, notice how the music in E minor has a key signature of G major? The two keys are closely related. We say that E minor is the *relative minor* of G major. In fact, the E minor blues scale we just played can also centre on G and be played in G major. It has a much brighter feel.

Here's a riff using the same notes, but in G major. It uses sixteenths, many of which are on the offbeat. Sixteenths are counted "one-ee-and-a two-ee-and-a" etc., which is written '1 e + a 2 e + a' etc. Count steadily out loud in sixteenths to play this blues-funk style riff accurately:

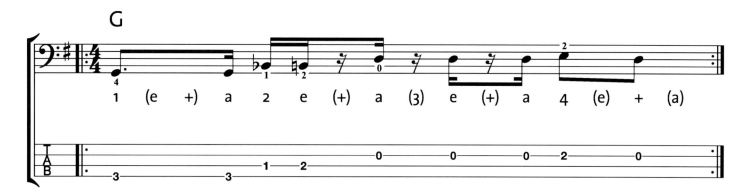

ROCK RIFFS

The electric bass has established itself nowhere more comprehensively and profoundly than in rock music.

The solid combination of bass and drums has become synonymous with rock and its sub-genres such as blues-rock, jazz-rock and heavy rock. Lets explore some of the key techniques.

The first adjustment to make is quite fundamental. It's time to use a pick. A pick isn't absolutely imperative for rock music, but there's no real reason not to take advantage of the edge to the tone that a pick gives. It creates a more immediate attack to the beginning of the note than fingertips alone can.

Grasp your pick lightly but firmly between the thumb tip and first finger as shown, leaving just enough pick protruding to strike the string accurately.

Let's take a look at a typical rock bass line. It has even eighths and—although it looks straightforward—playing eighth notes steadily and precisely is quite a knack. Move the pick alternately down and up across the strings, aiming to create an entirely solid wall of notes.

If you want to play in a convincing fashion, perfectly constant eighth notes will make all the difference.

Notice also, by the way, that we now have a *tempo marking*.

The number next to the quarter note symbol at the start of the music indicates the number of beats per minute that the piece should be played to.

Use a metronome or drum machine to set the speed (you can get inexpensive electronic metronomes at any music shop).

Rock music tempo instructions are often very precise, and being able to play steadily at a given speed is a key skill for a rock bassist.

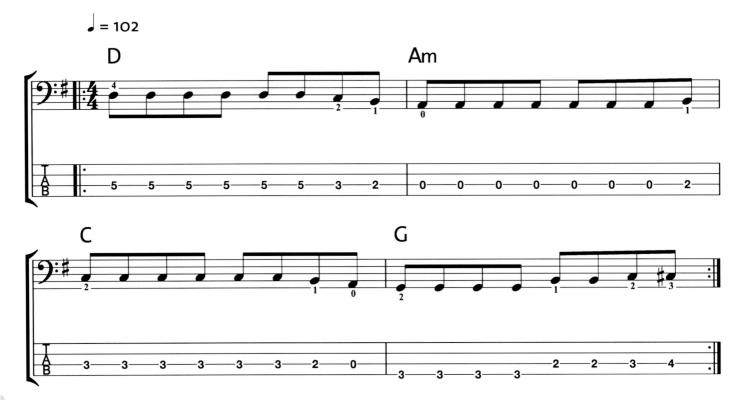

Now here's a variation on the same sequence. This time there is a new musical symbol to mention.

The bowed line joining two notes of the same pitch—as for example the middle of bar one—is a *tie*. It's just a way of displaying a note not easily indicated with a single symbol.

In general, notes are not beamed between one half of the bar and the other, making rhythms easier to follow. So this quarter note is shown as two *tied* eighths—but played as a standard quarter.

Aim to play the notes *on* the beat with a down-pick and those *off* the beat (the 'ands') with an up-pick. You should always be picking down on the beat. It'll help you to keep the rhythm flowing and the pulse constant.

When playing tied eighths be sure to keep the pick moving down and up even if you're not picking. It'll ensure you're in the 'correct' position when the tie is finished. Use the same fingering position as the previous example.

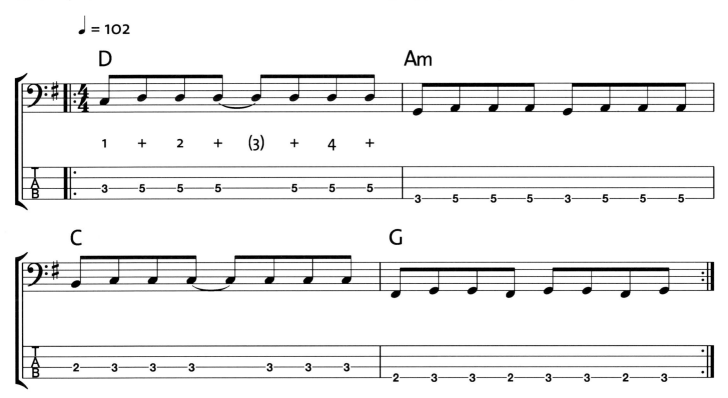

Finally, another variation on the same sequence. This one has rests. Practise picking down on the beat and up off the beat: you will need to move the pick in the rest and during the quarter notes too. You'll find it helps you to play the rhythm accurately. Count out the eighths if you're struggling to play the off-beat notes.

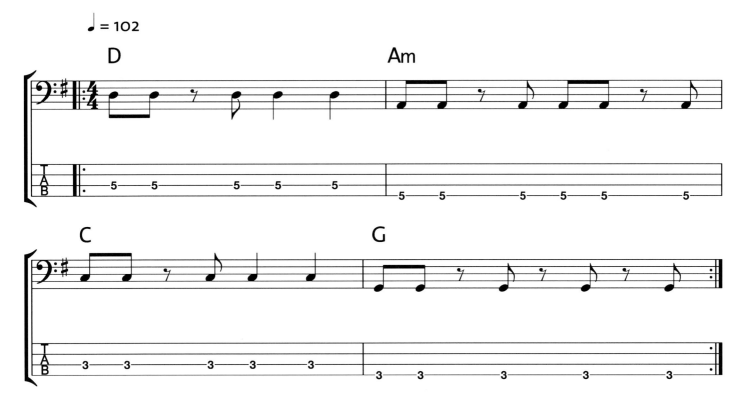

LATIN STYLES

Latin American music is a vast subject, but in Western dance repertoire it boils down to the Brazilian *bossa nova* and *samba* and from Cuba the *salsa* and *cha-cha-cha*.

In Latin American music, rhythm is the thing. Invariably originating with dance music, the vibrancy of the styles is built on rhythmic patterns, and the bass part is at the centre of these rhythms.

Many jazz players incorporate elements of Latin styles into their playing, but it's not difficult to get something of the flavour of these genres by following a few basic guidelines. We'll look at syncopation (displacing accents) and some key characteristics of each style.

These examples will give you an idea of what is going on, but the only way to really understand this music is to check out lots of recordings of Brazilian and Cuban music and Latin jazz.

BOSSA NOVA

The traditional bossa rhythm stems from the *claves* beat. This pair of resonant wooden rods plays a constant two-bar phrase (right) known as the *3/2* rhythm for the way the notes are divided.

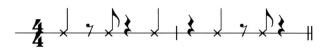

The bass typically plays the root and fifth, so your knowledge of alternating bass will come in handy!

Although written in four-to-the-bar, bossa nova is 'felt' as two beats: hence the metronome marking. Play with strong accents on 1 and 3, but don't overdo it.

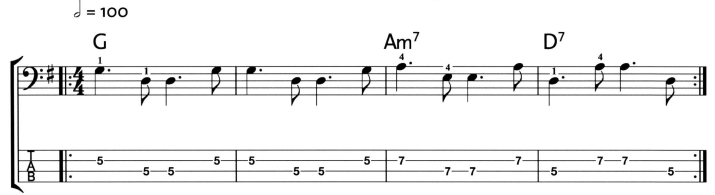

SAMBA

Played faster than the bossa nova, the samba rhythm is more dynamic. It includes tied notes that anticipate the following bar and decorative passing notes. In tab, only the first note of a tied group is shown.

These syncopated notes can be accented to give the rhythm even more energy. Be sure to lock into the bass drum rhythm. Here's a sample. Notice the time signature of 2/2—the rhythm is strongly felt in two-to-the-bar.

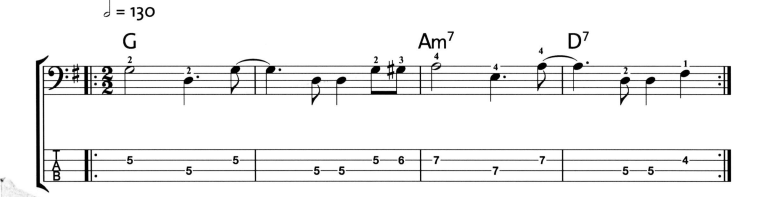

CHA-CHA-CHA

In the cha-cha-cha, the claves rhythm of the bossa nova is inverted and played as 2/3 (below).

The cha-cha-cha is a relatively recent dance form popularised by ballroom dancing and refined by various Afro-Cuban influences. Authentic cha-cha-cha phrasing begins on the fourth beat (dancers count "four-one-two-three"!) which takes a bit of getting used to.

In the example below, the fourth beat is tied over to the first. Count steadily and don't take it too fast.

Experiment with accents on beat 4 until you're happy with the amount of syncopation.

SALSA

Perhaps the most elusive of Latin styles, 'salsa' means different things to different people. However, all agree that it's an up-tempo Cuban dance form. Originating in the 1970s, salsa mixes easily with jazz and pop to create hybrid forms, too.

Driven by claves and a regular cowbell beat, salsa typically includes eighth note anticipation for each half-bar—the bassist rarely plays on 'one'. This relentless anticipation requires practice, but once you can play it without having to count the beats, you'll be much more relaxed!

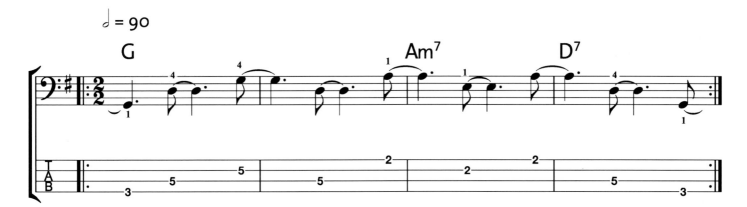

REGGAE STYLES

At the heart of reggae is the combined textures of syncopated drumming and heavy, solid bass lines. Reggae covers a multitude of styles, but they all share this common characteristic.

Reggae grew out of ska, an up-tempo dance with heavy accents on two and four.

Ska itself has its roots in calypso—which can clearly be heard in ska bass lines. We'll look at ska, reggae and the more modern development, dub.

SKA

Ska bass lines tend to contain alternating bass notes, arpeggiated chords and walking bass too. In fact, the techniques studied in this book give you all you need to play authentic ska-style bass.

What sets ska apart, however, is the solid four-in-the-bar bass part juxtaposed against syncopated guitar strumming and drums providing a heavy *backbeat* on the snare drum on beats 2 and 4.

Here's an example using arpeggios. Play the quarter notes very evenly:

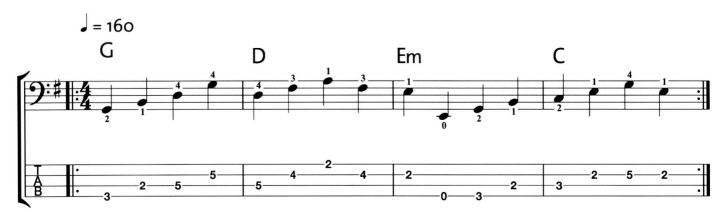

REGGAE

Reggae is always played in four-to-the-bar, but the eighths can be swung, especially in up-tempo tunes.

The drums and bass together are referred to as the *riddim* as exemplified by Robbie Shakespeare and Sly Dunbar.

Drummers often play a style called 'one drop' in which the first beat is left entirely empty, creating lots of space.

Good reggae playing has to do with resisiting the temptation to fill the space created between the bass and the drums with extra notes. Let the rhythm speak for itself—it's surprising how sparse reggae bass lines can be.

Try this Robbie-inspired line using lighly swung sixteenths, paying particular attention to the spacing between the notes: their exact length is a crucial part of the timing.

Here's a straightforward reggae line that syncopates the first beat. Leaving the first eighth silent like this gives the bass line a bouncy feel.

Try it straight, as written, or else try it with swung eighths. With swing, the bounce is even more evident.

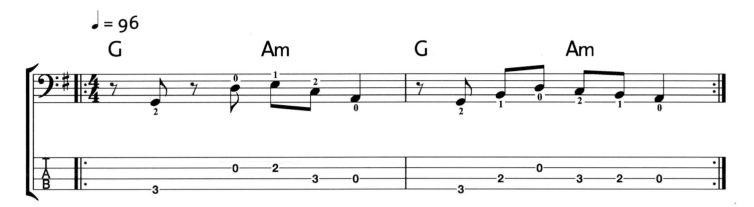

Reggae has fused successfully with rock in various ways. The Clash, for example, integrated reggae-style drum patterns and bass lines into their punk rock guitar sounds.

Here's a riff reminiscent of Paul Simonon's influential sound. Play it as heavily as possible, making sure you don't get ahead of the beat.

DUB

Originating among key reggae producers such as Lee 'Scratch' Perry, the dub genre grew out of remixing existing recordings, emphasising the bass to sound prominent in lo-fi sound systems.

This bass line needs to be played very steadily, with the tone controls of the bass amp set to boost the low frequencies—aim for an almost booming timbre. Consider ear protection if you get seriously into dub.

FUNK STYLES

The rhythmic groove of funk comes from the combination of bass and drums. Funk compositions often have very simple chord sequences but complex rhythmic elements.

Let's kick off with a line reminiscent of Bootsy Collins' work with James Brown, à la 'Sex Machine'. This riff is built on sixteenths which need to be played snappy and short.

Consider playing the strings down towards the bridge pick-up to create more bite to your sound (right).

Notice also the bowed line like a tie on the final beat. Pick the A, then bring the fretting finger for B down hard to sound the note without re-picking the string.

This is known as a *hammer on*—it's very useful for joining fast sixteenths, in fact many funk bass lines depend on it.

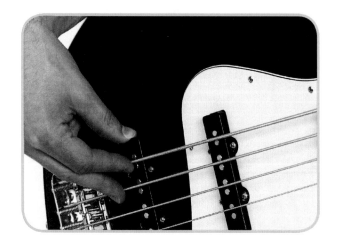

You'll soon develop a feel for the most important notes relative to your current position. On the left, the 1st finger is placed on G at the 3rd fret, bottom string, and the 4th finger is poised two frets (and two strings) higher—an octave away. Meanwhile, notice that the 3rd finger is ready to play D, the fifth.

Whether you're playing walking bass, alternating bass, reggae, latin or funk... this hand position will allow you to locate not only the octave and fifth, but any neighbouring notes too.

This means you can confidently find notes without looking, giving you more freedom to listen to the music you're playing.

And here's a syncopated sixteenth pattern in the style of James Jamerson or Jaco Pastorius. Again, play down at the bridge. If you're struggling with the timing, count out loud.

Notice the 'x' notes: these are *ghost* notes. The note is played without indistinct pitch. Play the written note but fret it loosely, muting the note as soon as it sounds.

DISCO

Disco is a specialised genre that grew out of funk. For the bassist, disco generally means a constant eighth-note rhythm, often in octaves—as is in this example.

To play recurring octaves like this with confidence, you'll need to adopt a left-hand postion like the one shown opposite. It'll really help your technique.

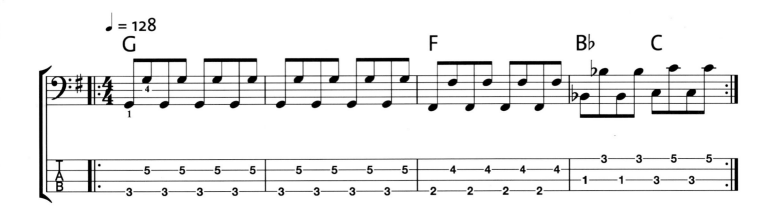

BASS GUITAR: WHO'S WHO

Here's a list of musicians to check out. It's always worth hearing the leading exponents in any genre, and there are plenty of other players out there who aren't on this list—it's just a taster.

The list also includes acoustic double bass players from the world of jazz. Electric bass players can benefit greatly by listening to double bassists!

POP

Nathan East (Eric Clapton, Phil Collins etc.)
Paul McCartney (The Beatles etc.)
Carol Kaye (1000's of sessions, Beach Boys etc.)

Sting
Mark King (Level 42)
Mike Mills (R.E.M.)

ACOUSTIC JAZZ

Paul Chambers (Miles Davis etc.)
Ray Brown (Oscar Peterson etc.)
Ron Carter (Miles Davis etc.)
Richard Davis (Eric Dolphy etc.)

Charlie Haden (Ornette Coleman etc.)
Charles Mingus
Milt Hinton
Dave Holland (Miles Davis etc.)

ELECTRIC JAZZ

Jaco Pastorius (Weather Report, Joni Mitchell, solo)
John Patitucci (Chick Corea etc.)
Victor Bailey (Weather Report, Joe Zawinul etc.)
Jeff Berlin (solo)

Stanley Clarke (Return to Forever, solo)
Steve Swallow (Carla Bley etc.)
Laurence Cottle (Laurence Cottle Big Band etc.)

SOUL

James Jamerson (Motown sessions)
Donald 'Duck' Dunn (Stax sessions)
Willie Weeks (Donny Hathaway etc.)

Chuck Rainey (Steely Dan etc.)
Bob Babbitt (Motown sessions)

FUNK

Larry Graham (Sly And The Family Stone, Graham Central Station etc.)
Marcus Miller (Miles Davis, solo)
Bootsy Collins (Parliament, Funkadelic etc.)

Bernard Edwards (Chic)
Nathan Watts (Stevie Wonder)
Anthony Jackson (Chaka Kahn etc.)
Francis 'Rocco' Prestia (Tower of Power)

ROCK

John Paul Jones (Led Zeppelin)
John Entwistle (The Who)
Jack Bruce (Cream)

Flea (Red Hot Chili Peppers)
Billy Sheehan (Mr Big, Steve Vai etc.)
Les Claypool (Primus)

REGGAE

Aston 'Family Man' Barrett (The Wailers)
Robbie Shakespeare (Sly & Robbie, innumerable sessions)

Bill Laswell (legendary producer and bass player)
Ronnie McQueen (Steel Pulse)

LATIN

Rather than following specific bass players, to really get a feel for Latin music you need to hear examples by prominent artists and band leaders. Here are a few:

Cha-Cha-Cha: Orquesta Aragón, Xavier Cugat
Bossa nova: Antonio Carlos Jobim, João Gilberto
Samba: Paulinho da Viola, Bola Sete
Salsa: Rubén Blades, Tito Puente